A Search Institute Report

Boxed In and Bored:

How Middle Schools Continue to Fail Young Adolescents—And What Good Middle Schools Do Right

Peter C. Scales, Ph.D.

Acknowledgments

Many thanks to Dr. Dale A. Blyth, Jennifer Griffin-Wiesner, Eugene C. Roehlkepartain, and Kate Tyler, of Search Institute, and to Dr. Thomas S. Dickinson of Indiana State University for their careful reading of earlier drafts and their helpful suggestions for revision.

This report is based in part on Search Institute's framework of developmental assets, which undergirds the institute's national Healthy Communities • Healthy Youth initiative. Financial support for Healthy Communities • Healthy Youth is provided by Lutheran Brotherhood, a not-for-profit organization offering financial services and community service opportunities nationwide, as well as philanthropic outreach in communities.

Boxed In and Bored: How Middle Schools Continue to Fail Young Adolescents— And What Good Middle Schools Do Right

By Peter C. Scales, Ph.D.
Copyright © 1996 by Search Institute

10   9   8   7   6   5   4   3

Search Institute
700 South Third Street, Suite 210
Minneapolis, MN 55415
(612) 376-8955
1-800-888-7828

ISBN: 1-57482-365-5

Editor: Kate Tyler
Graphic Designer: Connie G. Baker

Printed on recycled paper in the United States of America

Table of Contents

1. Healthy Communities, Healthy Schools:
   Places Where Young People Thrive 5

2. Young Adolescents' Developmental
   Characteristics 15

3. Unleashing the Power of Young Adolescents:
   Middle Schools and Developmental Assets 29

4. A Final Word..41

Chapter 1:   Healthy Communities, Healthy Schools:
Places Where Young People Thrive

he old "junior high" many Americans remember attending is fast becoming a relic of the past. Schools organized as grades seven to nine have rapidly dropped in number over the past twenty-five years, as schools organized as grades six to eight have become the places where most young adolescents ages ten to fifteen go to school (McEwin, Dickinson, and Jenkins 1996). Along with the change in grade span has come a change in what many educators understand should be the recommended practices of middle schools. More and more middle schools are trying to provide environments, curricula, and instruction that fit well with young adolescents' developmental characteristics.

And yet, despite progress, too many young adolescents (research suggests as many as half) feel boxed in and bored in their middle schools: boxed in because their opportunities seem too few, and bored because they have neither sufficient supportive adult relationships nor sufficient curricular challenge to feel that school is a welcoming and exciting place to be. This is at odds with young adolescents' distinct cognitive and psychosocial needs. Middle school experiences are critical in determining young people's academic success and social behavior. Research suggests that schools, parents, and the rest of the community must do more to make middle schools places where young adolescents thrive.

One measure of this is the mixed progress made on the National Education Goals established in 1989 (National Education Goals Report 1994). On the positive side, the dropout rate among African Americans and whites of similar socioeconomic classes is now nearly the same (Schmidt 1995). Less encouraging however, is that the overall percentage of nineteen- and twenty-year olds who have completed high school was essentially unchanged by 1993 (87 percent versus a baseline of 86 percent), and dropout rates for poor and

Latino/Latina youths were still markedly higher (Students staying in school...1994).

A reason for hope is that the performance of thirteen-year-olds (eighth-graders) in the United States on normed achievement tests in mathematics and science have gone up. Unfortunately, scores in reading and writing have not (Students staying in school... 1994). After years of decline, cigarette smoking and marijuana use among eighth-graders rose significantly between 1991 and 1994 (Carnegie Council on Adolescent Development 1995). Moreover, there has been essentially no change in the proportion of tenth-graders who experience student behavioral disruptions that interfere with teaching and learning (National Education Goals Report 1994).

More and more educators, parents, policy makers, and researchers have concluded that early adolescence is the "last best chance" (Carnegie Council on Adolescent Development 1989) to significantly influence in a positive way the paths that adolescents take in their development. This includes adolescents' relations with family and friends, their connections to community, and their enjoyment of and success at school. As more attention has focused on this age group, more and more is being learned about what young adolescents need and how middle schools can most effectively equip young adoelscents for life.

The structure and curriculum in many—perhaps most—middle schools continues to be out of synch with young adolescents' developmental needs.

While more is known and being learned, much of this knowledge is not being put into practice in too many middle schools. For a variety of reasons, the structure and curriculum in many—perhaps most—middle schools continues to be out of synch with young adolescents' developmental needs. This report examines recent research and explores its implications for how middle schools operate. We also suggest remedies—based on new comprehensive research on asset development in young people—to help middle schools and communities become healthier, more nurturing, and more successful environments for youth.

▼ Young Adolescents and Early Adolescence Defined

We need first to agree about what we're discussing. At any given time from now to the early years of the twenty-first century, roughly one in twelve people in the United States will be a young adolescent.

Educators and researchers use varied age ranges to define the period of "early adolescence," including nine to thirteen, ten to fourteen, eleven to fifteen, twelve to fifteen, and ten to fifteen. Search Institute defines early adolescence as the period from ages ten to fifteen because those ages roughly mark the beginning and end of a set of physical, socioemotional, and cognitive changes. These chronological age markers are only approximate, because the changes occur at different times among young people. Children ages ten to fifteen generally are in grades five through nine; although the grades six-through-eight middle school is the most common school for young adolescents (and the one we refer to most often in this report), grades five and nine are important transition years. Increasingly, educators recognize that the transitions out of elementary school into middle school, and from middle to high school, are two of young adolescents' most vulnerable periods.

▼ The Invention of Adolescence

Until the mid to late 1800s in Europe and the United States, people did not generally recognize adolescence as a separate stage of life. Indeed, the developmental needs of both children and adolescents were given short shrift. Most children did not go to school; they worked as soon as they were physically able. Marriage at age ten, twelve, or fourteen was not uncommon, indeed, it was deemed necessary, given that many people died in their twenties and thirties.

Not until the last half of the nineteenth century did the notion begin to take hold of a distinct developmental stage between childhood and adulthood. The industrial revolution was changing the nature of work, and economists were reporting a connection between prolonged schooling and higher earnings. Schools were beginning to be organized by age groupings. The birth of the field of pediatrics focused attention on children's health, while the young field of psychology began to influence understanding of human development.

As the developmental stage was recognized, adolescence was perceived as a period of turbulence. Psychologist G. Stanley Hall, often called the "father of adolescence," wrote in the early 1900s of the "storm and stress" characteristic of "normal" development during the teenage years. Although the view of the teenage years as inherently turbulent was later debunked, this view—along with the data suggesting a positive value for more years in school—helped separate adolescence from adulthood both in concept and in practice (Kett 1993).

The emergence of the junior high school in the 1920s and again in the 1940s reflected a growing recognition among educators that younger adolescents were somehow different from older teenagers. Despite the intent of the earliest junior high pioneers to create a school that truly responded to the developmental realities of young adolescents, the junior highs familiar to most Americans largely remained a miniature version of the high school, treating young adolescents more or less as smaller versions of older youth.

Not until the early 1960s, with the beginnings of the middle school movement, did experts begin to re-examine the junior high school model in light of emerging research on young adolescent developmental needs, coming full circle back to the hopes of the pioneers in the 1920s. Those voices were, however, small in number. Further, while research on adolescence increased in the late 1960s and early 1970s, stimulated by federal initiatives at the National Institute of Child Health and Human Development and the now-defunct Office of Child Development, adolescence was still under-studied compared with early childhood.

This lack of attention was particularly true of early adolescence. By the late 1970s, Joan Lipsitz (1977) could conclude that early adolescence was the most "severely neglected" stage of adolescence, being "hardly studied and...underserved." These conclusions led her to found the Center for Early Adolescence at the University of North Carolina-Chapel Hill (1978–1995) to heighten national awareness among educators, youth workers, and others about the issues affecting young adolescents in their families, schools, and communities.

In excellent middle schools, there had to be evidence of student joy, as demonstrated by "laughter, vitality, interest, smiles, and other indications of pleasure."

In 1984, Lipsitz published *Successful Schools for Young Adolescents*, a seminal work based on case studies of four schools that had met "threshold" criteria for excellence, including scores on normed achievement tests at or above the school district's mean; low absenteeism of students and staff, low vandalism, minimal graffiti, and a low level of student suspensions; high parent satisfaction; and a reputation for excellence. To these criteria, Lipsitz added another, more elusive criterion: In excellent middle schools, there had to be evidence of student *joy,* as demonstrated by "laughter, vitality, interest, smiles, and other indications of pleasure" (15).

Since that time, there has been an "explosion" of research about adolescence (Petersen, Richmond, and Leffert 1993). During the past decade especially, there has been commensurate growth in research about early adolescence and interest in young adolescents. The reform of middle schools had been accelerating since the late 1970s, but picked up even more steam with the 1989 publication by the Carnegie Council on Adolescent Development of *Turning Points: Preparing America's Youth for the 21st Century*. That report identified a "developmental mismatch" between what young adolescents need and what most schools provide. The result has been a spate of improvements in how middle school teachers are trained and how schools are organized. But as many as one-third to one-half of middle schools have not changed much from the junior highs that spawned them, resulting in too many ten- to fifteen-year-olds who are neither academically nor socially prepared to achieve at high levels in school and to lead healthy lifestyles.

▼ Recommended Middle School Practices

Gaps still exist in understanding how context, culture, and environmental change affect young adolescents. Myths persist about what normal early adolescence is like. Recognition of the age group as a distinct developmental stage is still far from universal (for example, the federal government still reports education statistics mostly for "elementary" and "secondary" levels without reference to a "middle" level (Scales 1992). And many schools have been slow to take both the easy and difficult steps that research shows are necessary for a more positive school experience in early adolescence.

The good news is that there has been significant progress in the past 25 years. Slightly more than half of middle schools seem to be using practices that are exactly what experts say is needed for excellence. Challenging courses for all students, interdisciplinary curriculum, teacher teaming, opportunities to explore, comprehensive health education and a healthy school environment, and a more personalized school climate that provides rich adult guidance and connection with family and community are among the key recommendations of reports such as *Turning Points* and key professional middle school organizations such as National Middle School Association (1996).

There are encouraging signs of progress. In a study of nearly two thousand middle level schools, McEwin, Dickinson, and Jenkins (1996) found that 60 percent of middle schools now use an interdisciplinary curriculum. About half now have a teacher-based guidance program. And special programs to help students make the transition from elementary to middle school are common.

According to recent research, middle schools that put these practices most fully into effect have students who achieve more, behave better, and have higher self-esteem than students in other, more traditional schools. For example, in a report based on a study of thirty-one Illinois middle schools involving more than fifteen thousand students and nearly nine hundred teachers, Felner et al. (1996) report that sixth- and eighth-graders' mathematics, reading, and language achievement scores are highest for students in middle schools that most fully implement recommended practices. These successful schools have four or five common planning times per week for teachers on teams, not more than 120 students per team, no more than twenty to twenty-five students per teacher, and teacher-student advisory periods four or five times per week. Illustrating the challenge for school change, only nine of the study's thirty-one schools reached that level of implementation.

Yet many gaps remain. Too often, neither curricular design nor teacher or administrator training has kept pace with research into young adolescents' educational needs. For example:

◆ Fewer than half of middle schools have exploratory programs of ungraded and varied "minicourses," interdisciplinary teacher teams, and teacher-based guidance of advisory programs (Valentine et al. 1993).

◆ "Direct instruction" by the teacher (including lecturing and other teacher-telling rather than student-discovery methods) remains the primary mode of teaching (McEwin, Dickenson, and Jenkins 1996).

◆ One in three middle schools is now larger that the four hundred to eight hundred students recommended for establishing a personalized school atmosphere (McEwin, Dickenson, and Jenkins 1996).

Checklist of Recommended Middle School Practices

National Middle School Association, the leading voice for professionals and others interested in the education of young adolescents, recommends that middle schools have the following to be responsive to ten- to fifteen-year-olds (National Middle School Association 1995). We have added the examples to the original.

A caveat is in order: As Felner et al. (1996) observe, checklists can be misleading. Just becasue a school "has" one of these features does not necessarily mean it has the feature to the degree necessary to promote positive academic and behavioral outcomes among students. It also might have the feature but not other equally necessary features, so that it is just an isolated example of excellence rather than a description of the environment. Finally, a school might have a feature or even several recommended features, but not have been doing these for a sufficiently long time (at least five years) for a real change to be expected. A checklist is just a fleeting glance, not a deeply revealing examination, of a school's realities.

Developmentally responsive middle schools are characterized by:

♦ educators committed to young adolescents
(for example, specially trained teachers and administrators)

♦ a shared vision

♦ high expectations for all
(for example, minimal use of ability-grouping/"tracking")

♦ an adult advocate for every student

♦ family and community partnerships
(for example, family resource centers; service- learning programs; parent volunteer program)

♦ a positive school climate
(for example, safety; peer mentoring programs; cooperative learning)

Therefore, developmentally responsive middle schools provide:

♦ curriculum that is challenging, integrative, and exploratory (for example, interdisciplinary themes; exploratory mini-courses)

♦ varied teaching and learning approaches (for example, team teaching; service-learning)

♦ assessment and evaluation that promote learning (for example, "authentic" assessment based on student portfolios and projects; evaluation of personal progress, not only relative standing to peers)

♦ flexible organizational structures
(for examples, small "houses" or teams of faculty, staff, and students; block scheduling)

♦ programs and policies that foster health, wellness, and safety (for example, extensive health and sexuality education courses; peer mediation programs; teacher modeling of healthful exercise and nutrition habits)

♦ comprehensive guidance and support services (for example, teacher-based guidance programs; family counseling services)

Why have the gains in developmentally responsive middle school organization and curricula, although encouraging, still left so many schools treating young adolescents as either younger children or older teens?

A good measure of the answer is that most middle school teachers have had little specialized training. But the lack of training is itself driven by a teacher licensing system that, in most states, still does not recognize the middle school level as a separate and distinct level worthy of a separate and distinctly focused preparation program. In states where the middle level is recognized as unique, specialized middle-level training is more available (Scales and McEwin 1994).

In turn, the teacher licensing system is deeply affected by the political debates about standardized test scores and the expertise teachers have in particular, discrete subjects (as contrasted with their facility across several subject areas). An interdisciplinary, exploration-centered, personalized school environment is hardly what this system is likely to produce, yet that is exactly what young adolescents need.

ew middle school teachers, and even fewer principals, have been specially and comprehensively trained to work with this age group. Just one in five middle school teachers say they received any undergraduate training in key middle level practices before they became teachers, and even fewer receive a comprehensive, in-depth preparation for teaching young adolescents (Scales and McEwin 1994; Scales 1992). Even when masters-level preparation is added in, nearly half of middle school teachers still have not had a specialized background in how to teach ten- to fifteen-year-olds. And, "in the vast majority of states," anyone with a principal's license can lead a middle school, whether they have middle level training or not (McEwin and Dickinson 1996, 7).

A study of more than two thousand middle school teachers (Scales and McEwin 1994) found that those from more comprehensive preparation programs feel more adequately prepared and are more likely to have a license focused solely on the middle grades rather than a license that includes teaching other grades (e.g., kindergarten to twelve, kindergarten to eight, or six to twelve). Yet most states still allow middle level endorsements or "add-on" licenses that permit elementary- or high school-certified teachers with just a bit of extra training to teach middle school.

This is not an effective way to prepare teachers who deeply understand young adolescents and how schools, curriculum, and instruction should be organized to best teach them (Scales and McEwin 1994). A recent report on how middle school teachers should be prepared did not recommend the numbers of credit hours teachers should have, but the recommended comprehensiveness of the curriculum, field experience, and student teaching in middle schools could hardly be accomplished in just one or two specialized courses (McEwin, et al. 1995)

Moreover, few middle-level educators have been trained how to collaborate effectively with families and with their colleagues in community organizations to create healthy communities for youth development in which all community institutions and citizens are mobilized to care for and about youth. Good schools can do much to strengthen young people's developmental foundation, but it is exceedingly difficult to be a good school in an unhealthy, uncaring, fragmented community, or in isolation from the families and communities that make up the rest of young people's worlds (Scales 1995).

▼ Boxed In and Bored

The net result of this slow progress is that too many middle school students too often feel boxed in and bored. Too many young adolescents are lectured to just when they need to explore and interact in small groups. Too many are left without effective guidance and connections with caring adults just at the time when their physical, emotional, social, spiritual, and cognitive selves are undergoing great change. Too many are given curriculum that is less challenging and rules that are more strict than they experienced in elementary school, just when they need more academic challenge and a greater sense of participation in developing and enforcing the rules that regulate their behavior.

What Lipsitz (1984) found more than a decade ago is still true: Successful schools for young adolescents base all procedures, all policies, all practices, on a deep understanding of early adolescent development, especially the great variations within individuals and across individuals of the same chronological age. Knowing what the latest research says about early adolescent development is the first step in ensuring that schools —and communities— adjust to and become more challenging and supportive places for young adolescents.

Chapter 2: Young Adolescents' Developmental Characteristics

oung adolescents are experiencing a period of change more rapid than at any time other than infancy. The onset of puberty and the related changes in young adolescents' physical, socioemotional, and cognitive development produce at times dramatic differences in how these young people feel, think, and act. Any group of twelve-year-olds, for example, might include young people who are as young as nine or as old as fifteen in some aspects of their development. Any single twelve-year-old might feel, think, and act like a nine year old today, a twelve year-old yesterday, and a fifteen-year-old tomorrow. That same twelve-year-old might reflect those differing levels of maturity in a single day, but in differing situations, which call for differing developmental abilities. He or she might be able to run as fast as one would expect a twelve-year-old to run, be able to solve a difficult mathematics problem that is intended for a fifteen-year-old or ninth-grader, and also have the social reasoning of a nine-year-old when disappointed by a best friend. Young adolescents are highly variable.

Given the uneven development of young adolescents, understanding and flexibility are needed from the adults who love and care for them, including parents, teachers, and youth workers. New York City school principal Deborah Meier has written (1992) that we work best with those whose worst characteristics we find amusing—educators who find young adolescents to be amusing will go far.

▼ Physical development

Research Limitations

Until recently, most adolescents studied have been white, middle class, and male (Spencer and Dornbush 1990). As a result, much of what we "know" about adolescence has ignored the experiences of poorer youth, young women, and adolescents of color. Researchers have suggested that African American youth tend to experience the events of puberty earlier than European-heritage adolescents (Hayes 1987; Jackson and Ott 1989). Our knowledge of development among African American youth and other adolescents of color is spotty, however, limiting the usefulness of our research base.

New research has, however, replaced old ways of thinking about some adolescents. For example, we used to think that rural youth were pubertally delayed, compared with urban youth (Tanner 1978), but more recent studies suggest those differences never existed or no longer exist, and that rural youth, like their urban counterparts, may experience puberty earlier than their suburban peers (Robertson et al. 1992).

Puberty and Its Effects

"If infancy has its 'terrible twos,' then early adolescence has its 'terrible toos': too much, too little, too slow, too fast"

In Western cultures, girls generally grow up physically faster than boys, although the timing of puberty varies tremendously within each sex (and the meanings attached to puberty vary enormously across cultures—Gibbons 1993). For European-heritage females, breast-budding begins at about ten years (with a range from eight to thirteen years) and the first menstruation occurs at about twelve years. The first menstruation generally occurs after girls have completed their peak growth spurt. For males, the key biological markers occur about two years later, with testicular enlargement occurring between ages nine to thirteen, the peak growth spurt occurring around age thirteen (ranging between eleven and sixteen), and the first ejaculation around ages twelve to fourteen (Ott and Jackson 1989). These gender differences in the timing of physical puberty also presage a difference in the timing of social and intellectual puberty between the sexes.

Both girls and boys are more concerned with their looks and physical attractiveness during early adolescence than they were when younger. According to Search Institute's research (Benson, Williams, and Johnson 1987), nearly four in ten boys and six in ten girls in sixth grade worry "a lot" about their looks, with the figures rising to 50 percent of boys and 66 percent of girls by the ninth grade. It is clear that "if infancy has its 'terrible twos,' then early adolescence has its 'terrible toos': too much, too little, too slow, too fast"

(Scales 1991, 9). Young adolescents tend to be highly critical of themselves, as they begin to compare themselves—physically, cognitively, socially—with their peers and with the largely unattainable status of society's icons such as superstar athletes and models. Puberty heightens all these concerns as it causes some children to suddenly look more mature than their years, and others to appear delayed.

The fact of puberty is a primary reason why health education is so important for middle school youth. Young adolescents need opportunities to learn and ask questions about their bodies, their feelings, sexuality, and human development in general. They need to be able to learn about physical development and sexuality in a reassuring environment that stresses how broad the range of "normal" development really is.

Early and Late Maturation

The great age range of puberty means that many young adolescents are developing (or, perhaps more important, perceive themselves to be developing) earlier or later than their peers of the same chronological age. The research is not completely consistent, but early pubertal development seems to have a more positive affect on boys and a more negative one on girls.

Early developing girls report lower self-esteem than their later-developing peers (Petersen 1993; Richards and Larson 1993) and appear to have higher levels of dissatisfaction with their bodies, as well as a greater prevalence of eating disorders (Smolak, Levine, and Gralen 1993). Early physical development also can lead to earlier exposure to sexual relationships (Robertson et al. 1992). Young girls whose bodies look mature and who are involved with boys two to three years older (the most common pattern) rarely have either the emotional or cognitive maturity or the social wits necessary to successfully negotiate sexual situations and to handle the complex feelings they generate. Yet, because early adolescence is filled with contradictions and variability, these early-maturing girls emotionally may feel as if they are more mature than their later-developing peers and that they should be treated as such by parents, teachers, and other adults, including being granted more freedom. Precisely the opposite seems to happen (Eccles et al. 1993), however. Early-maturing girls report a tightening of rules rather than a loosening of them, both at home and school. The combination of being overmatched with sexually more experienced and canny young men, and (in their eyes) over-monitored by parents and teachers may be a contributor to these girls' feeling victimized and unworthy.

In contrast, early maturing boys may find that with their larger size and deeper voices they are treated with more respect by both other boys and adults, results that surely contribute to enhanced self-image. Unlike girls, (who tend to dread their first sexual experience), boys typically look forward to their first sexual encounters (Scales and Beckstein 1981). Like early-maturing girls, however, early-maturing boys also initiate sexual activity earlier than their later-developing peers, and so run greater risks than their peers of negative physical and emotional consequences from sexual activity for which they are emotionally and cognitively too immature (Irwin 1993).

Adult Reactions to Puberty

For both boys and girls, adults' reactions to puberty can be problematic. One study of 105 white, middle class families that included a sixth grader found that families with more physically developed children had more parent-child conflict, fewer overall positive relationships, and more worry about their children. Parents with early maturing adolescents also predicted they would have less future influence over their children than parents whose children were less well developed (Freedman-Doan et al. 1993).

Young people's perceptions of adults' attitudes toward them shift noticeably in the pubertal years, making it all the more important for adults to intentionally communicate positive feelings of support toward youth. The Minnesota Youth Poll found that 49 percent of children in elementary school believe adults think more negatively than positively about them, but fully 71 percent of young adolescents feel that way (Hedin 1988). In Search Institute's study of five thousand Minneapolis youth, just twenty-one percent felt that the community as a whole valued adolescents (Benson 1996). Young people's perceptions of adults' attitudes are not far off the mark, according to research by Midgley, Feldlaufer, and Eccles (1989). They reported that teachers of seventh-graders in a junior high school (compared with teachers of sixth-graders in an elementary school) trust young adolescents less, believe more strongly that they need to control and discipline these students, and have less belief in their own effectiveness as teachers.

Socioemotional Development

The distrust that many adults have toward young adolescents, and adults' desire to control them, are out of synch with young adolescents' socioemotional development. Indeed, many adults set extra limits on young adolescents precisely when they need more opportunities to be trusted and to make decisions.

Inherited Myths

The Society for Adolescent Medicine's Study Group on the Psychosocial Context of Adolescent Development pointed out that research concerning adolescents has been "preoccupied" with how they become independent and separate from parents and other adults, to the serious neglect of understanding the importance of adolescent attachments and interpersonal relationships (Irwin and Vaughan 1988). As a result, too much training for teachers and others who work with young adolescents has emphasized adolescents "breaking away" from parents and not enough has stressed their need for continued (although redefined) connection with parents and unrelated adults.

From the earliest days of twentieth century adolescent psychology, professionals and the public alike also have inherited persistent, but unfounded, beliefs that 1) turmoil between adolescents and their parents is normal and inevitable; 2) friends invariably unite with the adolescent against her or his parents; 3) adolescents ride an emotional roller coaster that makes the teenage years a particularly unstable period of life; and 4) psychological problems and loss of self-esteem should be expected.

Widespread belief in these myths means that regular or frequent adolescent emotional disturbances and behavior problems might be overlooked as "normal" and as something that young people will grow out of. On the contrary, these are signs of serious trouble that warrant counseling and other mental health support. Belief in these myths also helps maintain a negative image of adolescence as an upsetting time for adults as well as youth.

Research conducted since the early 1980s clearly has shown the belief in a turbulent adolescence to be wrong. Patterns of psychiatric disorders do change during adolescence, with adolescents more prone than younger children to depressive disorders involving suicidal thoughts and persistent impairment in their relationships, and more likely to experience eating disorders (Rutter 1990). But, 80 percent of adolescents negotiate this period either smoothly or with relatively minor emotional problems (Offer, Ostrov and Howard 1989).

Of course, some conflicts do increase during adolescence between parents and children, but both parents and young adolescents rate their general relationship quite highly (Scales 1991). And even though girls are more likely than boys to "lose" some self-esteem and have depressed moods, especially during early adolescence, self-esteem generally increases over adolescence as a whole (Petersen et al. 1993). In short, "normal adolescent development is a positive process" (Petersen 1993, 4; Irwin and Vaughan 1988; Feldman and

Research conducted since the early 1980s clearly has shown the belief in a turbulent adolescence to be wrong.

Elliott 1990). Highly publicized recent studies of girls' self-esteem have important weaknesses—either they derive from very small samples (e.g., Brown and Gilligan 1993) or they have research method problems (e.g., American Association of University Women, 1992). The latter study did not follow the same girls over time to see how self-esteem changed, but compared different girls who were at different ages.

The Balancing Act Between Connection and Distance

Young adolescents simultaneously want to belong to a group and to regulate themselves. They vacillate between wanting to exert their unique identity and to blend invisibly into the crowd. They want attention, guidance, and even supervision from adults, but not necessarily with their friends watching. It is a rare parent of a thirteen-year-old who has not been asked to walk some distance behind them so parent and young adolescent will not appear to be together. In a real sense, the job of a parent or caring adult is to keep inviting young adolescents to be close and keep giving them opportunities to do things together. In short, if you are a parent, teacher, or other caring adult, keep giving young adolescents the chance to reject you—and then do not take it too personally when they sometimes do so!

Young adolescents want to be accepted by a group of peers, especially a group that is well-respected by other young adolescents. Research has shown that even young adolescents who get into trouble for their behavior at school want to have conventional friends who are respected by others (Gillmore et al. 1992). They want to know that people other than their parents—both peers and other adults—care for them. This desire to socialize with peers can provide positive energy for student success when teachers use cooperative learning strategies, activities that call on small groups of students to work together on problems.

Young Adolescents' Three Psychosocial Questions

Am I competent? Am I normal? Am I loveable and loving?

Psychoanalyst Erik Erikson suggested a framework for human development that described each life stage as having particular psychosocial "crises" to resolve. Young adolescents might be said to be asking themselves three psychosocial questions that correspond to Erikson's crises of establishing a sense of industry, identity, and intimacy (Erikson 1968): Am I competent? Am I normal? Am I loveable and loving? (Scales 1991). Some days the answers to these questions are reassuring and some days they are not, and young adolescents' emotional responses can vary commensurably. Whether at home, in school, or in community settings, the job of adults is to ensure that all young adolescents can answer "yes" to these questions. This is not always easy, because young adolescents' search for themselves and for what to believe can cause them to push, test, and challenge adults.

Exploring and Experimenting

During early adolescence, young people need to find out what activities they like and what they are good at doing. Exploration is their developmental work, much as playing is the developmental work of infants and young children. Young adolescents need many opportunities to discover their talents, interests, and values.

Because this is a time when young adolescents are trying on for size different attitudes and values no less than different styles of dress and varied activities, they may appear to be especially argumentative with adults, disagreeing with adult values on various political, religious, or social issues. Real differences of opinion might exist, of course, but often, young adolescents argue a position to understand themselves better more than to convince adults of the validity of that position. "Sometimes they appear to be figuring out what they believe—at least for the moment—by listening to themselves talk about themselves" (Stevenson 1992, 84).

Changes in young adolescents' cognitive abilities increasingly allow them to see exceptions, contradictions, and gray areas in life choices, which can be unsettling when compared with the certainty with which they understood the world when they were younger. Not being sure how to relate in newly changing, more ambiguous circumstances and relationships—whether with parents, teachers, other caring adults, peers, or romantic friends—can lead young adolescents to confusing behaviors that include alternation of "anxiety and fear with reassuring bravado, shyness with noisiness, and over-responding with fear to (sic) respond" (National Middle School Association 1992, 10).

Of course, very real risks are associated with this exploration and experimentation. But we might consider that risk = developmental exploration + environmental danger. Some risk taking is a normal part of adolescent development. One theory of adolescent risk taking hypothesizes that stress and boredom (along with a biological predisposition to sensation seeking) are at the heart of risk-taking behavior (Levitt, Selman, and Richmond 1991). Other research has shown that adolescents' decisions about risk taking more often are influenced by the desire to experience something fun than by the fear of experiencing negative consequences (Maggs, Almeida, and Galambos 1995). Thus, simply stressing the risks involved in certain behaviors such as early sexual intercourse or using drugs is by itself not a very effective prevention strategy.

> *Girls who develop earlier than their peers may be at an added disadvantage in a traditional junior high setting because of the discrepancy between how they want to be treated, based on their view of themselves as increasingly mature, and how they experience being treated.*

The responsibility of teachers, parents, and other caring adults is not totally to prevent risk, for that would mean preventing the developmentally necessary exploration young adolescents need. Rather, the task is to reduce risk by reducing environmental danger. This is accomplished by providing critical developmental assets in young people's lives, such as surrounding them with support from caring adults, setting boundaries and high expectations for behavior, providing plentiful opportunities to engage in constructive and empowering activities, and helping them develop a commitment to educational and core values such as behavioral restraint and the importance of helping others. These developmental assets are discussed in greater detail later.

The Impact of Simultaneous Changes

Researchers consistently report that young adolescents' emotional states are influenced not only by the physical changes of puberty, but also by the other changes in their lives. When pubertal changes occur at the same time as other important changes, such as transition from elementary to a junior-high-like school, the adolescent is more likely to experience greater negative emotional consequences, including lower self-esteem, school misconduct, and depression in mid-adolescence (Petersen et al. 1993; Petersen 1992; Feldman and Elliott 1990; Simmons and Blyth 1987). On the other hand, research shows that school transition can be positive when it is to a genuine middle school that effectively responds to young adolescents' characteristics and needs. For example, middle schools' use of team teaching that increases student-teacher intimacy seems to reduce the stress students feel as they change schools (Fenzel 1989).

Male and Female Vulnerability

Research suggests that girls are more vulnerable to emotional problems and boys to behavior problems during early adolescence (Ingersoll and Orr 1989), a finding that appears to be valid cross-culturally (Gibbons 1993). Girls experience pubertal development earlier than boys, and seem to react more adversely to the compounding effect of simultaneous family changes and school transitions (Petersen 1992; Forehand, Neighbors, and Wierson 1991; Simmons and Blyth 1987).

Girls who develop earlier than their peers may be at an added disadvantage in a traditional junior high setting because of the discrepancy between how they want to be treated, based on their view of themselves as increasingly mature, and how they experience being treated. Eccles et al. (1993) reported a study of fifteen hundred young adolescents who moved from the sixth grade in a kindergarten through sixth-grade school to the seventh grade in a seventh through ninth-grade junior high school. Physically mature girls were twice as likely as their later-developing peers to say they should have a say in determining things such as seating arrangements, class rules, and homework, but to claim that they did not have a say in these classroom decisions.

In fact, the early maturing girls said they had even less opportunity for decision making in the spring term than in the fall, while the later developers said they had more. Either teachers are treating early maturing girls differently, or the early maturers are experiencing similar teacher treatment differently, or both. In either case, the potential outcomes seem to include lower self-esteem, lower academic motivation, and greater dissatisfaction with school. If these girls feel they are capable of accepting more responsibility and challenge, and yet are provided with no more or even less of these opportunities to act mature, they may come to view themselves as not liked or incompetent, feelings which may contribute to a lowered sense of self-esteem.

Furthermore, the positive impact of a good middle school may be lower for girls than for boys. Fenzel (1989) discovered that the transition to a genuine middle school using team teaching is especially beneficial to boys. Although boys and girls in middle school had similar levels of stress, boys had less stress in a good middle school than they had in their elementary school. Fenzel theorized that boys may feel especially strained in an elementary school because their restless behavior is a mismatch with what he called the "feminized" climate of elementary schools, whereas good middle schools understand that restlessness is a normal part of early adolescence for both boys and girls.

▼ Cognitive Development

The Myth of Perceived Invulnerability

Young adolescents' cognitive skills are more concrete than abstract. They tend to think poorly about future consequences, and view situations primarily from their own rather than other people's perspectives. Until recently (Keating 1990), researchers had thought that young adolescents' egocentricity produced a sense of invulnerability that made them poor judges of potential life risks. But recent research has cast doubt on the assumption that these traits are peculiar to adolescents as a group. Rather, certain adolescents may be disposed to feeling invulnerable. For example, Quadrel, Fishoff, and Davis (1993) compared eighty-six pairs of low-risk adolescents and their parents, recruited through public schools, with ninety-five high-risk adolescents, recruited from group homes for teens with legal and chemical abuse problems. They found that the high-risk teens were overconfident of their abilities to avoid consequences such as unplanned pregnancy and auto-crash injury. The low-risk teens (a population in which "invulnerability" should have been more normally distributed) and the parents did not differ from each other in the degree to which they thought they were personally susceptible to these events. Neither the low-risk youth nor their parents showed overconfidence. The researchers concluded from their own and others' studies that "there is very little empirical support for the claim that perceived invulnerability is particularly large during adolescence" (1993, 105). Susan Millstein (1993) agreed, although she observed that research in this area is too sparse to draw solid conclusions one way or the other.

The Capacity for Abstract Thinking

Accepted developmental theory argues that young adolescents steadily progress from a more concrete to a more abstract reasoning capacity (Keating 1990). Abstract thinkers are able to imagine hypothetical situations, reconcile contradictions, envision exceptions, and predict long-term consequences of immediate behavior. However, the reality of how young adolescents develop intellectual capacity—like most of what we know about young adolescents—appears to be more complicated than generally has been thought.

Young adolescents need to be challenged. "Most evidence" suggests that delaying cognitive challenge "may actually be harmful" (Keating 1990, 63). During early adolescence, young people's cognitive ranges do expand. Like the rest of their development, however, the growth of these abilities is inconsistent, variable, and situation-specific. Young adolescents are more capable of imagining the future, generating hypotheses, drawing conclusions and justifying exceptions to rules than they were at younger ages. But how well they do varies with the specific circumstances in which they find themselves. They may do quite well, for example, in a social studies activity in which they imagine what society would be like if only wealthy, white males could vote, but do quite poorly in real life when deciding how to say "no" to sexual advances by someone who they want to turn down but still keep as a friend.

The cognitive differences between youth at the earlier and later ends of the early adolescence period were illustrated by a study of moral problem-solving. Adelson (1986) showed that young adolescents are more able to articulate and understand the needs of the larger group or community at fourteen and fifteen years old than at eleven or twelve. At the younger ages, they easily can see how an action affects them personally but cannot as easily take into account its impact on others. At the older ages of early adolescence, they are more able to understand how an individual sacrifice can lead to a larger benefit for the wider community. This may illustrate a difference in what motivates different ages of young adolescents to volunteer in their communities. At the younger ages, students may volunteer because it feels personally good. At the older ages, it may also be seen as an important way to fulfill an adult role of contributing to the larger community.

Capacity and performance are of course not the same. Adolescents do have cognitive abilities that are more sophisticated than previously thought, but not as complex as those suggested in laboratory studies. Keating (1990) notes that although higher-order thinking is attainable by young adolescents, evidence for this has come from controlled laboratory settings where the adolescent subjects have plenty of time to come up with responses. This setting is in sharp contrast to daily life, which often poses "time-limited, dynamic, and personally stressful cognitive challenges" (Keating 1990, 64).

Despite some educators' enthusiasm for the strategy of teaching general, content-free thinking skills, the evidence is that familiarity with content and subject matter is strongly related to sophistication in thinking skills (Keating 1990; Resnick and Klopper 1989). For example, the sexuality education curricula for young adolescents that most successfully contribute to delayed initiation of sexual intercourse or to increased use of contraception do not teach general decision-making approaches, but instead focus on skills specific to the sexual situations in which young people might plausibly find themselves. The curricula that focus on general decision making in hopes that this will transfer to highly stressful, real-life sexual decision-making circumstances simply do not work (Kirby et al. 1994).

Schools that respond poorly to young adolescents' developmental needs may ... limit young adolescents' cognitive performance.

Moreover, because young adolescents reason in more advanced ways with familiar material than with unfamiliar, they are more likely to display higher-order thinking with a theme-based curriculum that integrates subject matter than with a curriculum in which many different subjects are taught in a fragmented and unconnected manner. Young adolescents also are likely to revert to less mature ways of reasoning when they are under stress (Feldman and Elliott 1990).

Some schools inadvertently may create a vicious circle of underachievement. Schools that respond poorly to young adolescents' developmental needs may add to their stress. In turn, stress may limit young adolescents' cognitive performance, which in turn may convince teachers and other adults that they are not capable. Teachers may then expect less and provide less challenge, and young adolescents themselves may conclude they are not sufficiently gifted to do well in school. Research suggests that young adolescents begin to draw conclusions about their abilities and commonly conclude that people who have to work hard at school are not very smart (Urdan, Midgely, and Wood 1995; Wenzel 1989). Some students may give up academically as a means of preserving self-esteem; they may convince themselves and others that if they really tried, they could do well.

Self-Discovery and "Romantic Understanding"

Susan Harter (1990) has reported that roughly around the age of thirteen, young adolescents increasingly are aware of inconsistencies in the various selves that they present to the world (what in the nineteenth century William James called "different me's"). They can discover, for example, that they present one side of themselves to parents, one to friends, one to adults they like, one to adults they dislike. Unlike younger children, they may be bothered by these inconsistencies. Because young adolescents are searching for truths in which to believe, the discovery that they themselves can be false and inauthentic can be especially troubling.

Young adolescents tend to be curious and are interested in exploring a wide range of issues, topics, and activities. They are attempting to understand themselves, to make sense of the world and their relation to it. They begin to think critically about the values they and others hold, especially parents and valued adults such as teachers. They are quick to detect hypocrisy in adults and often want to hear (and argue with) the justification for parental or other adult decisions.

Young adolescents are in the period that philosopher Alfred North Whitehead described as one of "romantic understanding" (Egan 1990). By that he meant the sense of wonder, excitement, and even awe that can be evoked as young people grasp the patterns in their lives and begin to connect disparate pieces of their lives together into a sensible whole. Middle schools that use inter-disciplinary, theme-based curricula may provide more interesting, less boring subject matter for young adolescents because connecting life's experiences to a meaningful whole is such an important part of the developmental work of ten- to fifteen-year-olds.

The Role of Controversy

One study of middle grades teachers found that teachers like young adolescents because they are beginning to think independently and complexly. Middle-level teachers get a lot of pleasure from seeing young adolescents experience the "sudden comprehension of content" when, as one teacher put it, the "light goes on" (Scales 1992, 66). This is the age when young people begin to wonder about and want to understand great themes such as power, justice, beauty, compassion, courage, and faith; when they can be deeply engaged by discussions of sex, race, gender, wealth and poverty, prejudice and privilege, and any number of moral and ethical issues found in current events. These are all "controversial" subjects. Despite their expanded intellectual interests, however, a study of twenty-five thousand eighth-graders reported that half are bored most of the time in school (Cross 1990). A recent study of a diverse group of students in nine high schools found much the same result: Forty percent of the twenty thousand students said they were just going through the motions in school (Steinberg, Brown, and Dornbush 1996). Part of the reason could be that many adults are afraid of talking about the very subjects that are the most interesting to young adolescents. Young adolescents thrive on content that includes some controversy.

Critical Thinking as an Attitude

Keating (1990) has written that critical thinking is a disposition or attitude as much as it is a skill. Where young adolescents are concerned, this presents some interesting challenges for many adults. Educators (and parents) face a contradiction in the curriculum and in development, for example, when they urge young adolescents to be critical thinkers in language arts and sciences, but in health and sexuality matters, to "just say no." Critical thinkers do not simply just say no; they do not just obey. Youthful critical thinkers challenge, test, prod, and push. They want to debate, ask for reasons, and they are interested in exploring "what if …?" possibilities.

What is normal young adolescent inquisitiveness can be perceived by some adults as nosiness in relation to personal matters. Adults might even consider young adolescents' questioning to be an irritating challenge to authority if it persists beyond the adults' interest in the subject being pursued or the time the adult has allotted to it. Moreover, adults who work with young adolescents must guard against gender, racial, and socioeconomic biases in these circumstances. Questioning and debate by a white, male, middle-class young adolescent might be welcomed as a properly assertive intellectual interest by some white, middle-class parents, teachers, or youth workers—who might perceive this same expression as a behavior problem, aggressiveness, or lack of control or respect if it comes from an African American or Latino male young adolescent, a young adolescent who is living near poverty, or a female young adolescent.

Chapter 3: Unleashing the Power of Young Adolescents: Middle Schools and Developmental Assets

 e have briefly described some of the physical, socioemotional, and cognitive characteristics of normal early adolescence. These characteristics tell us something about what young adolescents need from their environment so as to grow up to become healthy, caring, productive, and happy adults. They also underscore the positive possibilities of this age group, helping us understand how much young adolescents can contribute to their environment.

Young adolescents share with people in other age groups a number of basic human needs; they also have some needs that are especially crucial in their particular developmental stage. All people need to feel safe and have a sense of structure and coherence in their lives. All people need to belong to a group, or several groups. All people need to feel self-worth, a sense of control over their own lives, a closeness in at least one sustained relationship, and a sense of competence. Young adolescents especially need to have varied opportunities to explore themselves and their environments. They need a lot of physical activity, a balance between supervision and clear limits, and increasing opportunities to participate meaningfully in their schools, families, and communities (Dorman 1985; Pittman and Wright 1991; Scales 1991).

All these needs are reflected in a framework developed by Search Institute. The Institute's studies of more than 250,000 sixth- through twelfth-graders in more than 460 urban, rural, and suburban U.S. communities has yielded a framework of developmental assets, or essential building blocks, that youth need to become healthy, caring, and productive adults (Benson 1996; Benson, Galbraith, and Espeland 1995; Benson 1993). In this framework, external assets are the relationships and opportunities adults provide that help young people develop internal assets, the values and skills they will need to guide themselves for the rest of their lives. (See Figure 1.)

Figure 1

Developmental Asset Categories

External Assets	Internal Assets
• Support	• Educational commitment
• Empowerment	• Values
• Boundaries and expectations	• Social competencies
• Constructive use of time	• Positive identity

The purpose of promoting critical developmental assets for young people is not simply to help prevent or reduce negative outcomes, but to promote positive goals. In broad terms, the aim is to help young people become adults who are healthy, caring, productive, and happy.

Positive goals include measures of *thriving* such as succeeding in school (getting mostly As), contributing to community (performing community service one hour or more a week), believing in the value of racial diversity, having a plan to go to college, and being optimistic even in the face of frustration. The more assets young people experience, the more likely they are to attain these positive goals. The average youth, however, has fewer than half of these assets (Benson 1996; Benson 1993).

Middle schools play a critical role in promoting adolescent asset development. For example, twenty-three of the forty developmental assets in Search Institute's framework can be directly affected by young adolescents' experiences in middle schools. (See Figure 2.) Many of the others could be influenced indirectly.

Figure 2

40 Developmental Assets*

Support

1. Family life provides high levels of love and support.

2. Parents and youth communicate positively; youth is willing to seek parents advice and counsel.

3. *Youth receives support from three or more non-parent adults.*

4. Youth experiences caring neighbors.

5. *School provides caring, encouraging environment.*

6. *Parents are actively involved in helping children succeed in school.*

Empowerment

7. Youth perceives that community adults value young people.

8. Youth are given useful roles in community life.

9. *Youth gives one hour or more per week to serving in her/his community.*

10. *Youth feels safe in home, school, and community.*

Boundaries and expectations

11. Family has clear rules and consequences; and monitors whereabouts.

12. *School provides clear rules and consequences.*

13. Neighbors would report undesirable behavior to family.

14. Parent(s) and other adults model prosocial behavior.

15. Youth's best friends model responsible behavior.

16. *Both parents and teachers encourage youth to achieve.*

Constructive use of time

17. *Youth is involved three or more hours per week in lessons or practice in music, theater, or other arts.*

18. *Youth is involved three or more hours per week in sports, clubs, or organizations at school and/or in community organizations.*

19. Youth is invovled one or more hours per week in religious programs or services.

20. Youth spends two or fewer nights per week out with friends "with nothing special to do."

Educational commitment

21. *Youth is motivated to do well in school.*

22. *Youth has a B average or better.*

23. *Youth reports one or more hours of homework per day.*

24. *Youth cares about her/his school.*

25. *Youth reads for pleasure three or more hours per week.*

Values

26. *Youth places high value on helping others.*

27. Youth places high value on promoting equality and reducing hunger and poverty.

28. Youth acts on convictions and stands up for her/his beliefs.

29. *Youth tells the truth even when it is not easy.*

30. *Youth accepts and takes personal responsibility.*

31. *Youth believes it is important not to be sexually active or to use alcohol or other drugs.*

Social competencies

32. *Youth has skills to plan ahead and make wise choices.*

33. *Youth has empathy, sensitivity, and friendship skills.*

34. *Youth has knowledge of and comfort with people of differing racial/ethnic backgrounds.*

35. *Youth can resist negative peer pressure.*

36. *Youth seeks to reduce conflicts non-violently.*

Positive identity

37. *Youth feels he/she has control over "things that happen to me."*

38. Youth reports high self-esteem.

39. Youth reports "my life has a purpose."

40. Youth is optimistic about her/his personal future.

* *Assets middle schools can directly affect are in italics*

As schools provide the external assets—support, empowerment, boundaries and expectations, and constructive use of time—they enable young adolescents to develop the internal assets—educational commitment, values, social competencies, and positive identity—that will help them guide themselves.

▼ Themes Connecting Assets to School Success

The asset framework and recent research challenge us to reframe our thinking about young adolescents' capabilities and interests, and about how schools, parents, and communities should respond. We believe that, to unleash the power of young adolescents to be active learners and community citizens, schools and communities need to tap into young adolescents' potential excitement about learning, their sense of exploration and discovery, their new capacity to see the needs of others, and their desire to make a contribution to society. Successful schools build on young adolescents' assets in order to promote school success. (One tool for measuring whether a middle school is doing so is the *Middle Grades Assessment Program*, available from Search Institute.) Those young adolescents are more likely to succeed at school and thrive in other positive ways if they:

- ◆ are challenged and empowered to use their newly emerging cognitive skills to really think, and not just to parrot back facts;

- ◆ are exposed to thematic, team-taught interdisciplinary curricula that help them meaningfully connect content that has relevance in the real world beyond school;

- ◆ have families and teachers who set (and model) high expectations for achievement and personal behavior from them; have opportunities to serve and help others, offering their time and talents to make their communities better places in which to live;

- ◆ go to schools that strengthen their motivation to learn, not for the end of getting good grades, but for the end of experiencing joy, growth in capacity, and increased understanding of their worlds through learning (ironically, those youth will probably end up with better grades too);

and

◆ live in communities where schools, families, and other community resources work together to unleash the power of young adolescent idealism and energy, through such efforts as providing after-school opportunities, programs and activities that help parents with raising their children, and explicit efforts to develop a common vision, language, and values about nurturing children and youth.

How can schools provide each of the external assets to help develop this kind of empowering environment?

Support

Support—caring relationships with family and unrelated adults—is perhaps the single most important asset young adolescents can have. The bottom line is that all young people need at least one adult who has what Bronfenbrenner (1991) has called an "irrational emotional attachment" to that child. This is the feeling that the child is special, wonderful, and precious, no matter what the objective data are to the contrary: "it is the illusion that comes with love" (1991, 3).

In the literature on child development, it is clear that certain kinds of parent-child relationships are positively related to good outcomes, while others are not. Parents who are firm but loving ("authoritative"); who do not use physical punishment, but instead explain discipline and involve their young adolescent children in helping to set rules and punishments; and who spend time having fun with their children, have young adolescents who engage in less delinquent behavior and have higher levels of self-esteem, better attitudes toward school, better grades, less substance abuse, and less sexual activity than parents who are either too strict or too permissive. In a sample of about ten thousand adolescents and their parents, researchers found this to be true regardless of whether families were headed by one or two parents, were rich or poor, or were African American or white (Steinberg et al. 1991).

Caring relationships with unrelated adults also are important in much the same ways. The literature is limited, but it suggests that young adolescents see unrelated adults such as teachers, coaches, religious youth workers, and neighbors more frequently than family adults other than parents. These unrelated adults can assume greater importance as the adolescent ages. Moreover, for some adolescents in some settings (such as middle schools), they might be especially critical influences, depending on the young person's race, gender, age, socioeconomic status, and educational plans. These unrelated adults may become more important because they can provide advice for particular youth (e.g., teachers for college-bound adolescents) or because they

Young people need at least one adult who has what Bronfenbrenner has called an "irrational emotional attachment" to that child.

can provide similar support but even more autonomy than parents feel comfortable granting (Scales and Gibbons 1996).

Unfortunately, according to Search Institute's research, only 36 percent of young people feel that school is a caring place (reanalysis of Benson, 1993). There is enormous room for improvement here. As we discussed earlier, young adolescents socioemotional development might be said to involve questions that respond to Erik Erickson's developmental tasks of industry, identity, and intimacy. Good middle schools enable young adolescents to answer "yes" to the psychosocial questions: "Am I normal? Am I competent? Am I loveable and loving?" (Scales 1991). They adjust the school environment so that it responds to what ten- to fifteen-year-olds actually are like.

The dropout rate is just one of the stubborn education challenges parents, schools, and communities face. Disengagement with school—disinterest, boredom, and a lack of connection—is common, with 40 percent of high school youth and nearly 50 percent of middle school youth reporting such disengagement (Steinberg, Brown, and Dornbush 1996; Cross, 1990).

All the dropout prevention and school reform literature can be reduced to a single conclusion: Young people are more likely to stay in school and do well there (or any other program) if they like it there. And they are more likely to like middle schools if they feel safe there, if they have successes there, if their friends, neighbors, and family are proud of what they do there, if they have fun there, and if they feel someone in the school cares for them.

Good middle schools build intimacy and connection and give all students a sense that they are cared for. They have a smallness of scale, through arranging schools with hundreds of teachers and students into much smaller teams. They use team teaching and block scheduling to reduce the number of class changes and teacher changes young adolescents have to make each day. Such structural stability is important to middle school youth, whose socioemotional and cognitive capacities are in flux. Young adolescents whose teachers are in teams typically mention how teams improve teacher-student *relationships* even more than they mention the activities they do in their teams (Kramer 1992).

Good middle schools have teacher-based guidance and advisory programs, and they extensively use various cooperative learning strategies that allow teachers to act as coaches to small groups of students—instead of as classroom lecturers to thirty youth who are discouraged from talking with one another. Good middle schools understand that nurturance is not incompatible with high academic performance and that, for many youth, it is a prerequisite. Although school nurturance may be even more important for youth who lack parent and extended family support, all youth benefit from a caring school environment. It should not be surprising that another Search Institute study of 112 communities found that youth in the healthiest communities (i.e., communities with fewer youth engaging in problem behaviors) were significantly more likely to feel their schools were caring and encouraging places (Blyth and Leffert 1995).

Recent research has shown that all of these practices are necessary for positive academic and behavioral outcomes to occur among students. Team sizes that are too big (more than 120 students), student/teacher ratios that are too large (above twenty-five), and common teacher team planning periods that are too few (fewer than four per week) each are associated with middle school students feeling more negative about school, having more mental health and behavior problems, and achieving at lower levels (Felner et al. 1996).

Empowerment

One in eight young people overall, and one in three in high-crime neighborhoods, say they have cut classes or stayed away from school because of crime and the fear of violence (Applebome 1996). Young adolescents are the most common age group to experience victimization, much of which—from robbery to fighting, to sexual harassment—occurs at school (Scales 1991). Yet, ensuring safety in schools goes beyond school and community policies and resources that keep weapons off school grounds and that enable young people to walk or ride unharmed to school.

Good middle schools take steps to train teachers in promoting nonviolent conflict resolution and train youths themselves to be peer mediators, an approach that research suggests may have its greatest impact at the middle school level (Cutrona and Guerin 1994). Psychologist Daniel Goleman (1995) made a good case for "emotional intelligence" being more important for success in life than cognitive intelligence. Emotional intelligence includes anger management and impulse control, empathy, and non-violent conflict resolution. Teaching and modeling these skills needs to be a school-wide emphasis, not only a unit in health class.

Safety is one empowerment asset directly affected by middle schools; another is community service. Providing service to others can help young adolescents feel they can make a valuable contribution to their school and community. Young people need to help build their community, not just live in it. Search Institute's research finds that as little as one hour per week spent helping others can dramatically lower young adolescents' risks. Helpers are more motivated to succeed in school, more involved with religious organizations, have friends who exert more positive than negative influences on them, and have more communication with adults other than their parents, when compared with young adolescents who don't help others to that degree (Benson 1993).

Unfortunately, young adolescents of both genders say they do less for others after a peak of helping at seventh grade; boys' level of helping others drops most during this time (Benson and Roehlkepartain 1991). Ironically, young adolescents' cognitive ability to appreciate the needs of others beyond themselves, the needs of their neighborhoods and communities, is increasing during the very years when they start giving less. This is most likely because adults stop asking them to contribute and fail to provide opportunities for them to help. The failure to ask may be a combination both of adults' discomfort or confusion over how to act with young adolescents, and an erroneous belief that youth need to "break away" from adult influence as part of the normal development of "independence." For example, in a Search Institute study of more than 650 workers in family support programs nationwide, nearly 40 percent believed, incorrectly, that young adolescents need "a lot" of independence from adults (Scales 1996).

Diane Hedin's (1988) observation from research with thousands of youth is pertinent here. It is plausible that "adolescents, by and large, view themselves as ever more competent, independent, and capable, while they contend (with a good deal of justification) that adults view them as increasingly irresponsible and immature" (1988, 39). As discussed earlier in relation to early-maturing girls and self-esteem, it may be that as young adolescents develop more maturity, they focus on how far they've come, and see the potential for more responsibilities and privileges, whereas adults focus on how far they still have to go, and see the need for continued or in some cases even greater strictness and oversight.

Good middle schools give young adolescents the chance to regulate more of their lives. Plentiful adult supervision and guidance is provided, but young adolescents contribute to the development of the rules and punishments for their behavior in school, enjoy a free student press that encourages rather than suppresses coverage of controversial issues, and have many opportunities to serve their communities.

The best middle schools do not only enable young adolescents to serve, but also integrate the experiences into the curriculum; students think, read, and communicate about the service they have contributed. Good middle schools promote the widespread use of *service-learning* as a teaching and learning strategy. Service-learning can enable young adolescents to feel they have important roles in bettering their school and community. It can also make students feel closer to one another and to teachers. One Illinois school, for example,

The best middle schools do not only enable young adolescents to serve, but also integrate the experiences into the curriculum.

has used service-learning as a key component of its advisory program (Kurth 1995). By performing service together, and discussing its meaning together, these students and teachers understand each other more and become more likely to see the values and interests they share, that is, their common interests rather than their differences. In the process, students' bonds to schools are likely to be strengthened.

The experiential aspect of service-learning also may provide an especially powerful means of demonstrating to underachievers that they too can have success at school. But what sets service-learning apart from mere community service is how well integrated service is with the core curriculum. In a good service-learning program, students spend considerable time and effort reflecting and communicating about the connection of their service activity to the academic content they are studying.

Boundaries and Expectations

High expectations have a clear impact on academic performance. For example, in a longitudinal study that followed 110 white, upper middle-class girls from middle to high school, researchers reported that mothers' attitudes toward their middle school daughters' involvement in math were strongly associated with daughters' math grades later in high school. Mothers' own attitudes about math did not seem to matter much. Nonetheless, if a mother thought that her middle school daughter had good math ability, believed that math was important for her daughter, and expected her daughter to do well, the daughter was much more likely to have higher grades in math during high school (Klebanov and Brooks-Gunn 1992).

The importance of high expectations also is illustrated in a twenty year follow-up study of 254 children born to African American, "relatively disadvantaged" teenage mothers in Baltimore in the late 1960s (Brooks-Gunn, Guo, and Furstenberg 1993). Teen mothers who aspired to complete high school had children who developed similar aspirations; at eighteen, they were less likely to drop out of high school than were their peers. Furthermore, if these children aspired to post-high school education while they were still in middle school, their risk of dropping out was reduced dramatically by about 80 percent.

Good middle schools build a sense of competence by offering challenging curriculum based on setting high expectations for everybody. Accepting minimum standards for some young people because they have experienced great risk in their lives is unacceptable in a good middle school. To some degree, lower expectations of poor students and students of color has been a result of viewing cognitive growth as necessarily sequential, with students having to master "basic skills" before being exposed to more "advanced" or higher-order content. But new evidence from cognitive science has suggested instead that schools should focus on complex, meaningful problems and embed basic skills within more interesting and challenging content, supplementing this approach with more connections to students' out-of-school culture and using more dialogue than lecture (Means and Knapp 1991).

Good middle schools don't let minimum "floors" of achievement become young adolescents' ceilings. A recent study of 820 high schools and eleven thousand students shows the positive academic effects of using such practices, including mixed-ability grouping rather than tracking in math and science, interdisciplinary teaching teams, and a small-group, cooperative learning approach rather than lectures. These were high schools, but all those practices are recommended for middle schools as well. In those schools, students showed significantly greater gains between eighth and tenth grade in engagement with school and in achievement in math, science, reading, and history, whereas students in traditional schools showed decreases on all those measures, that is, they were more bored and less successful. Moreover, the achievement gap between students from higher and lower socioeconomic backgrounds was less in these restructured schools (Lee and Smith 1994).

Good middle schools also build a sense of competence through a wide-ranging program of exploratory courses and opportunities so that young adolescents can identify their own interests, talents, and values. In these schools, young adolescents are not boxed in to limited course content, but can experience a broad range of subjects and activities. Exploration and diversity of opportunities also build a sense of self-efficacy, an asset necessary for a positive identity. John Lounsbury (1991) has written that the curriculum of the middle school *is* exploration. Not all children initially do well with the kinds of intelligence (logical, verbal, and mathematical) primarily called upon in schools. Yet, if young people are to become and remain connected with schooling, they must regularly experience success in school. Some children have a musical intelligence, or a gift of body movement, or spatial intelligence, and others have an interpersonal intelligence that makes them outstanding leaders. Exploration of varied activities and subjects gives young people a chance to find out what it is they are good at, so that they can answer "yes" to the psychosocial question, "Am I competent?"

Good middle schools enable all students to experience challenging curriculum in an environment that rewards individual progress. They make minimal use of ability-grouping, a practice which the National Research Council flatly concludes "has not been shown to improve learning among low-achieving students" (1994, 111). They also stress "task" goals that emphasize learning for its own sake, as contrasted with "performance" goals that emphasize one's relative standing against others. Research shows that young adolescents in a highly competitive school environment give up more easily and attribute success to luck more than effort, and also feel less connected to school (Wentzel 1989; Zimmerman and Arunkumar 1994).

Good middle schools make life interesting in school not only through lots of exploratory activities but through theme-based, interdisciplinary curricula that link young adolescents' personal concerns with great philosophical, ethical, and social issues. Good middle schools include as a core part of their curriculum extensive opportunities for learning in life sciences and in health and sexuality education, because these are the areas in which young adolescents are experiencing some of the most fundamental and meaningful changes in their lives. Health represents one of the most sound developmental content areas around which to provide theme-based, interdisciplinary, thought-provoking curriculum (Scales 1993).

Constructive Use of Time

To promote resilience and reduce risk, young adolescents need access to structured community activities. Young adolescents who spend more than two hours a day unsupervised by adults after school during the school week are much more likely to engage in risky behaviors and do poorly at school than better-supervised children; at least 30 percent of the nation's eighth-graders find themselves facing that amount of time with nothing constructive to do (Carnegie Council on Adolescent Development 1992). Search Institute's data show that young adolescents who participate in structured activities such as after-school clubs, religious organizations, community service programs, and supervised camping and recreation programs, are much less likely than other youth to fail at school, use drugs, or engage in early sexual intercourse (Benson 1993).

Time spent participating in positive, productive activities can build other assets too. It promotes a sense of self-efficacy as young adolescents continue to discover that there are many things they are good at doing. It helps young adolescents learn critical social skills and identify their personal talents, interests, and values. It also is another way of building supportive relationships with caring adults and responsible peers who share positive values and provide role models. A study of more than four thousand students and 370 teachers and administrators found that students in middle schools that emphasize good connections with after-school activities have significantly higher socioemotional functioning and academic achievement than students in schools that do not as fully implement this middle school practice (Jackson et al. 1993). Recent research, however, has also cautioned that, just as students who work twenty hours a week or more suffer academically, youth who engage in extracurricular activities for twenty hours a week or more also show academic decline (Steinberg, Brown, and Dornbush 1996).

Good middle schools recognize that positive young adolescent development is best achieved when all parts of the young person's ecology are linked—that is, when schools, families, and communities collaborate. Collaboration means extensive parent and family participation with schooling, and rich connections between middle schools and community resources, from service-learning opportunities to school-based adolescent health services and family support programs, to after-school programs, religious activities, and neighborhood programs. Increasingly, researchers believe that promoting healthy communities rests in large measure on building "shared values and norms that will energize and hold together these adult networks and reinforce their authority and legitimacy with their youth" (Connell, Aber, and Walker 1995, 109–110). Communities that have strong bonds among their adults create a coherent social fabric for young people, increasing the chance of fostering positive development of young adolescents even in otherwise risk-filled circumstances.

Chapter 4:   A Final Word

All the educational reform one can imagine will be without impact unless middle school faculty and staff truly enjoy young adolescents and define them positively, unless parents participate in the life of the school, and unless community residents advocate for the systemic supports that make it possible for dedicated teachers and school staff to do their jobs well.

There is a lesson for us in looking at why some of our most challenged youth succeed. Researchers have found that youth are best supported by people with five characteristics:

◆ They see genuine potential in youth.

◆ They put youth at the center of their programs.

◆ They believe they can make a difference with youth.

◆ They feel they are contributing to the community something they owe.

◆ They are "unyieldingly authentic."

People with such characteristics are "wizards," in the words of the researchers, because they succeed in an environment where many do not (McLaughlin, Irby, and Langman 1994).

Young adolescents need teachers and principals who are wizards too. One who truly enjoys and has been specially prepared to teach young adolescents will describe them not as loud, nosy, naive, undiplomatic, stubborn, or unrealistic, but instead as energetic, curious, idealistic, honest, confident, and optimistic. Middle schools that are filled with such teachers, administrators, counselors, nurses, community resource people, and parents can be places where young adolescents feel challenged and nourished, where they have the optimism that comes from multiple opportunities, and the excitement that comes from exposure to new and personally meaningful experiences–where they don't feel boxed in and bored.

Our schools—and communities—need teachers and other adults with this shared vision: A willingness to meet young adolescents' on their own developmental terms. In realizing this vision, we will not merely help young adolescents get through this stage of life, but thrive. We will also tap our own idealism and energy, as we create schools and communities where young adolescents are full of joy and hope.

References

Adelson, Joseph. 1986. *Inventing Adolescence: The Political Psychology of Everyday Schooling*. New Brunswick, N.J.: Transaction Books.

Appelbome, Peter. 1996. Crime fear is seen forcing changes in youth behavior. *New York Times* (12 January): A6.

American Association of University Women. 1992. *Shortchanging Girls: Shortchanging America*. Washington, D.C.

Benson, Peter L. 1996. *Developmental Assets among Minneapolis Youth: The Urgency of Promoting Healthy Community*. Minneapolis: Search Institute.

——. *The Troubled Journey: A Portrait of 6th–12th Grade Youth*. Minneapolis: Search Institute.

——. and Eugene C. Roehlkepartain. 1991. Kids who care. *Source Newsletter* (Search Institute) 7(3): 1–3.

——. Dorothy Williams, and A. Johnson. 1987. *The Quicksilver Years: The Hopes and Fears of Early Adolescence*. San Francisco: Harper and Row.

Blyth, Dale A., and Nancy Leffert. 1995. Communities as contexts for adolescent, development: An empirical analysis. *Journal of Adolescent Research* 10: 64–87.

Bronfenbrenner, Urie. 1991. What do families do? *Family Affairs* (Institute for American Values) 4(1-2):1–6.

Brooks-Gunn, Jeanne, Guang Guo, and Frank F. Furstenberg, Jr. 1993. Who drops out of and who continues beyond high school? A 20-Year follow-up of black urban youth. *Journal of Research on Adolescence* 3(3): 271–94.

Brown, Lyn M., and Carol Gilligan. 1993. Meeting at the crossroads: Women's psychology and girls' development. *Feminism and Psychology* (February) 3(1): 11–35.

Carnegie Council on Adolescent Development. 1989. *Turning Points: Preparing American Youth for the 21st Century*. Washington, D.C.

___. 1992. *A Matter of Time: Risk and Opportunity in the Nonschool Hours*. Washington, D.C.

___. 1995. *Great Transitions: Preparing Adolescents for a New Century*. New York: Carnegie Corporation of New York.

Connell, James P., J. Lawrence Aber, and Gary Walker. 1995. How do urban communities affect youth? Using social science research to inform the design and evaluation of comprehensive community initiatives. In *New Approaches to Evaluating Community Initiatives*, ed. James P. Connell, A. Kubisch, L. Schorr, and C. Weriss. Washington, D.C.: The Aspen Insttitute, 93–125.

Cross, Christopher T. 1990. *Who is the American Eighth Grader?* Washington, D.C.: U.S. Department of Education, Office of Educational Research and Improvement.

Cutrona, Cheryl, and Diane Guerin. 1994. Confronting conflict peacefully: Peer mediation in schools. *Educational Horizons* 72(2): 95–104.

Dorman, Gayle. 1995. *The Middle Grades Assessment Program*. Reprint, revised by Robin Pulver. Minneapolis: Search Institute.

Eccles, Jacquelynne S., Carol Midgley, Allan Wigfield, Christy Miller Buchanan, David Reuman, Constance Flanagan, and Douglas Mac Iver. 1993. Development during adolescence: The importance of stage-environment fit on young adolescents' experiences in schools and in families. *American Psychologist* 48(2): 90–101.

Egan, Kieren. 1990. *Romantic Understanding: The Development of Rationality and Imagination, Ages 8–15*. New York: Routledge.

Erikson, Erik H. 1968. *Identity, Youth, and Crisis*. New York: W.W. Norton.

Feldman, S. Shirley, and Glen R. Elliott. 1990. Progress and promise of research on adolescence. In *At the Threshold: The Developing Adolescent*, ed. Shirley S. Feldman and Glen R. Elliott. Cambridge, Mass.: Harvard University Press, 479–505.

Felner, Robert, Peter Mulhall, Deborah Kasak, Anthony Jackson, Steve Brand, and Nancy Flowers. Forthcoming. The impact of school reform for the middle years: A longitudinal study of a network engaged in *Turning Points*-based comprehensive school transformation. In *Preparing Adolescents for the Twenty-First Century,* ed. R. Takanishi and David Hamburg. New York: Cambridge University Press.

Fenzel, L. Mickey. 1989. Role Strains and the transition to middle school: Longitudinal trends and sex differences. *Journal of Early Adolescence* 9(3): 211–226.

Forehand, Rex, Bryan Neighbors, and Michelle Wierson. 1991. The transition to adolescence: The role of gender and stress in problem behavior and competence. *Journal of Child Psychology and Psychiatry* 32(6): 929–37.

Freedman-Doan, Carol R., Amy J.A. Arbreton, Rena D. Harold, and Jacquelynne S. Eccles. 1993. Looking forward to adolescence: Mothers' and fathers' expectation for affective and behavioral changes. *Journal of Early Adolescence* 13(4): 472–502.

Gibbons, Judith L. 1993. *Adolescence in Cross-National and Cross-Cultural Perspective.* St. Louis: Department of Psychology, St. Louis University.

Gillmore, Mary Rogers, J. David Hawkins, L. Edward Day, and Richard F. Catalano. 1992. Friendship and deviance: New evidence on an old controversy. *Journal of Early Adolescence* 12: 80–95.

Goleman, Daniel. 1995. *Emotional Intelligence.* New York: Bantam Books.

Harter, Susan. 1990. Processes underlying adolescent self-concept formation. In *From Childhood to Adolescence: A Transitional Period?,* ed. R. Montemayor, G.R. Adams, and T.P. Gullotta. Newbury Park, Calif.: Sage, 205–39.

Hayes, Cheryl, ed., 1987. *Risking the Future: Adolescent Sexuality, Pregnancy, and Childbearing.* Washington, D.C.: National Academy Press, National Research Council.

Hedin, Diane. 1988. The view from inside: The Minnesota Youth Poll. *New Designs for Youth Development* 8(3): 32–39.

Ingersoll, Gary M. & Daniel P. Orr. 1989. Behavioral and emotional risks of early adolescence. *Journal of Early Adolescence* 9: 396–408.

Irwin, Charles E., Jr. 1993. Adolescence and risk taking: How are they related? In *Adolescent Risk Taking*, ed. N. J. Bell and R. W. Bell. Newbury Park, Calif.: Sage, 7–28.

___, and Elaine Vaughan. 1988. Psychosocial context of adolescent development. *Journal of Adolescent Health Care* 9: 11S–19S.

Jackson, Anthony W., Robert D. Felner, Susan G. Millstein, Karen J. Pittman, and Ramsay W. Selden. 1993. Adolescent development and educational policy: Strengths and weaknesses of the knowledge base. *Journal of Adolescent Health Care* 14: 172–89.

Keating, Daniel. 1990. Adolescent thinking. In *At the Threshold: The Developing Adolescent*, ed. Shirley S. Feldman and Glen R. Elliott, 54–90. Cambridge, Mass.: Harvard University Press.

Kett, Joseph F. 1993. Discovery and invention in the history of adolescence. *Journal of Adolescent Health Care* 14: 605–12.

Kirby, Douglas, Lynn Short, Janet Collins, Deborah Rugg, Lloyd Kolbe, Marion Howard, Brent Miller, Freya Sonenstein, and Laurie S. Zabin. 1994. School-based programs to reduce sexual risk-taking behaviors: Sexuality and HIV/AIDS education, health clinics, and condom availability programs. *Public Health Reports* 109(3): 339–60.

Kramer, Linda R. 1992. Young adolescents' perceptions of school. In *Transforming Middle Level Education: Perspectives and Possibilities*, ed. J. L. Irvin. Boston: Allyn & Bacon, 28–45.

Kurth, Barbara. 1995. Learning through giving: Using service learning as the foundation for a middle school advisory program. *Middle School Journal* 27: 35-41.

Lee, Valerie E. and Julia B. Smith. (1994). High school restructuring and student achievement. *Issues in Restructuring Schools* (University of Wisconsin, Center on Organization and Restructuring of Schools), Report No. 7: 1–5, 16

Levitt, Mira Zimansky, Robert L. Selman, and Julius B. Richmond. 1991. The psychosocial foundations of early adolescents' high-risk behavior: Implications for research and practice. *Journal of Research on Adolescence*, 1(4): 349–78.

Lipsitz, Joan. 1984. *Successful Schools for Young Adolescents*. New Brunswick, N.J.: Transaction Books.

__. 1977. *Growing up Forgotten: A Review of Research and Programs Concerning Early Adolescence*. Lexington, Mass.: D.C. Heath.

Lounsbury, John H. 1991. *As I See It*. Columbus, Ohio: National Middle School Association.

Maggs, Jennifer L., David M. Almeida, and Nancy L. Galambos. 1995. Risky business: The paradoxical meaning of problem behavior for young adolescents. *Journal of Early Adolescence*, 15(3): 344–62.

McEwin, C. Kenneth, and Thomas S. Dickinson, and Doris M. Jenkins. 1996. *America's Middle Schools: Practices and Progress, a 25-year Perspective*. Columbus, Ohio: National Middle School Assocation.

__, and Thomas S. Dickinson. 1996. *Forgotten Youth, Forgotten Teachers: Transformation of the Professional Preparation of Teachers of Young Adolescents*. New York: Carnegie Corporation of New York, paper prepared for Middle Grade School State Policy Initiative.

__, and Thomas S. Dickinson, Thomas O. Erb, and Peter C. Scales (1995). *A Vision of Excellence: Organizing Principles for Middle Grades Teacher Preparation*. Columbus, Ohio: National Middle School Association.

McLaughlin, Milbrey W., Merita A. Irby, and Juliet Langman. 1994. *Urban Sanctuaries: Neighborhood Organizations in the Lives and Futures of Inner-City Youth*. San Francisco: Jossey-Bass.

Means, Barbara and Michael S. Knapp. 1991. Cognitive approaches to teaching advanced skills to educationally disadvantaged students. *Phil Delta Kappan*, 73(4): 282–89.

Meier, Deborah. 1992. Perspectives on the 'new' middle school movement: The urban context. Speech to Carnegie Corporation of New York Middle Grade School State Policy Initiative National Workshop, 22 October.

Midgley, Carol, Harriet Feldlaufer, and Jacquelynne S. Eccles. 1989. The transition to junior high school: Beliefs of pre- and posttransition teachers. *Journal of Youth and Adolescence* 17(6): 543–62.

Millstein, Susan G. 1993. Perceptual, attributional, and affective processes in perceptions of vulnerability through the life span. In *Adolescent Risk Taking,*ed. N. J. Bell and R. W. Bell. Newbury Park, Calif.: Sage, 55–65.

National Middle School Association. 1991. *This We Believe.* Columbus, Ohio: Author.

——. 1995. *This We Believe.* Columbus, Ohio: Author.

National Research Council. 1993.*Losing Generations: Adolescents in High-Risk Settings.* Washington, D.C.: National Academy Press.

Offer, Daniel, Eric Ostrov, and Kenneth I. Howard. 1989. Adolescence: What is normal? *American Journal of Diseases of Children* 143: 731–36.

Ott, Mary Jane, and Patricia Ludder Jackson. 1989. Precocious puberty: Identifying early sexual development. *Nurse Practitioner* 14(11): 21–30.

Petersen, Anne C. 1993. Presidential address: Creating adolescents: The role of context and process in developmental trajectories. *Journal of Research on Adolescence* 3: 1–18.

——, Julius B. Richmond, and Nancy Leffert. 1993. Social changes among youth: The United States experience. *Journal of Adolescent Health* 14: 632–637.

——, Bruce E. Compas, Jeanne Brooks-Gunn, Mark Stemmler, Sydney Ey, and Kathryn E. Grant. 1993. Depression in adolescence. *American Psychologist* 48(2): 155–68.

Pittman, Karen J., with Marlene Wright. 1991. *A Rationale for Enhancing the Role of the Non-School Voluntary Sector in Youth Development.* Washington, D.C.: Center for Youth Development and Policy Research, Academy for Educational Development.

Quadrel, Marilyn Jacobs, Baruch Fischoff, and Wendy Davis. 1993. Adolescent (in)vulnerability. *American Psychologist* 48(2): 102–16.

Resnick, Lauren B., and Leopold E. Klopfer. 1989. Toward the thinking curriculum: An overview. In *Toward the Thinking Curriculum: Current Cognitive Research*, ed. Resnick and Klopfer. Washington, D.C.: Association for Supervision and Curriculum Development, 1–18.